Editor

Eric Migliaccio

Managing Editor

Ina Massler Levin, M.A.

Editor-in-Chief

Sharon Coan, M.S. Ed.

Illustrator

Blanca Apodaca

Cover Artist

Barb Lorseyedi

Art Manager

Kevin Barnes

Art Director

CJae Froshay

Imaging

Richard E. Easley
Rosa C. See

Product Manager

Phil Garcia

Publisher

Mary D. Smith, M.S. Ed.

Author

Laureen Reynolds

Teacher Created Resources, Inc.

6421 Industry Way

Westminster, CA 92683

www.teachercreated.com

ISBN 13: 978-0-7439-3507-4

ISBN 10: 0-7439-3507-1

©2004 *Teacher Created Resources, Inc.*

Reprinted, 2006

Made in U.S.A.

Table of Contents

Introduction 3
Activity Suggestions and Ideas 4
Student Book Cover 9
Pattern Pages 10
Poems
  "Adding" 12
  "All Of Us" 13
  "Almost Five" 14
  "At Recess" 15
  "Be A Friend" 16
  "Before Bed" 17
  "Bug and Bee" 18
  "Come Out" 19
  "Encouragement" 20
  "Friends" 21
  "Funny" 22
  "Grown-Up Wishes" 23
  "Guessing Game" 24
  "Hide and Seek" 25
  "I Like, I Can" 26
  "I Saw It" 27
  "Just Because" 28

  "Just Like Me" 29
  "Let's See (Sharing with a Crocodile)" . . 30
  "My Tree" 31
  "Not!" 32
  "Opposites" 33
  "Practicing" 34
  "Pretending" 35
  "The New Year" 36
  "The Sleepover" 37
  "The Story" 38
  "The Story Teller" 39
  "The Trip" 40
  "The Wish" 41
  "Things I Think" 42
  "Tree House Rules" 43
  "When Are We Going?" 44
  "Where Is The Cat?" 45
  "Who Are You?" 46
  "Wish Upon A Star" 47
  "You Can!" 48

Introduction

Welcome! Young children can become poetry lovers and yes, even poetry readers! Each poem in *Sight Word Poetry* was specially written with beginning and developing readers in mind. The poems are comprised primarily of words from the Dolch and Fry lists and have delightful rhyme and rhythm to entice young readers. Their predictability and repetition make them the perfect introduction to the world of poetry for students and teachers alike.

Why write a book of sight word poems? Sight words are the foundation of fluent reading. New readers encounter them 70–85% of the time in the first years of their reading careers and almost 65% of the time as mature readers. Readers who possess a solid sight word vocabulary spend less time grappling through text and more time gaining fluency, comprehension, and confidence. Becoming comfortable with sight words leads a reader to become comfortable with reading. By using poetry, educators can model fluency through their oral reading and encourage it in the low-risk environment of whole-group choral reading. Developing a foundation of sight words also helps young writers to communicate more creatively because their energy is spent on the expressive words, not on the connecting ones.

While the poems in this book are meant to be read and enjoyed, don't stop there! Use the activities and suggestions on the following pages to bring poetry into other areas of the curriculum, like math, science, social studies, guidance, and physical education. They can be used with more than one title, more than one time. Many activities also provide opportunities to address the different levels of achievement that inevitably exist in a classroom each year. Reading these poems will leave students wanting more, so encourage new readers by finding other collections that fit the bill. Writing poetry is also a natural extension to the reading. Start students off with poetry blanks where a skeleton of a poem is in place but blank spaces exist for individual ideas. Move on from there to free verse or name poems so a child's personality can truly shine through.

Most important of all, when using this book, have fun! Developing a true enjoyment of words at an early age will lead to a lifelong pursuit of books. There is a smile inside each poem, and each reader is just waiting to emerge.

Activity Suggestions and Ideas

✣ **Scavenger Hunt**

Have your students use multi-colored highlighters to locate specific words, rhyming pairs, vowels sounds, or whatever fits your curriculum. The children will enjoy using these "special" markers, and you will be able to check their progress at a glance.

✣ **Create Poetry Books**

Feature a poem each week. Begin on Monday and practice reading the poem with your students everyday. Include some of the activities from these pages during the course of the week. By Friday, each child will be comfortable with the poem and able to read it to a friend. They can then each cut out the poem, glue it into a book of blank pages, and illustrate it. By the end of the semester or year, they will each have a book of poems to take home that they can proudly read to their families.

✣ **Grab Your Partner**

Reproduce an appropriate poem from the book. Have each student practice it with a pre-selected partner for several days or longer. Ask the team to illustrate the poem and read it to the class. Each week another pair of students can be in the spotlight.

✣ **Stick To It!**

Write the poem on a large piece of chart paper and leave sticky notes nearby. Ask each child to write his or her name on a note and cover up a word he or she knows. Bring the group together and have each student uncover his or her word and "teach" it to the class. A variation on this activity is to have children cover up an unknown word and as you uncover it, say the word so everyone can benefit.

✣ **Color Me**

Many of the poems contain color words. If you write the poem on chart paper, write the color word in its own color. Students can also circle color words in the appropriate color if you give them a copy to keep.

✣ **Find the Number Words**

Several of the poems found in this book contain number words. If you reproduce the poem on chart paper, write the number instead of the corresponding word for beginning readers. Students can also write the number next to the word on a copy produced for them.

Activity Suggestions and Ideas *(cont.)*

✢ Read the Walls

Write poems on chart paper and post them around your room. Supply students with colorful pointers so they can practice reading them on their own. When introducing this activity it is important to model your expectations for pointer use so that they are used safely.

✢ Transparent Poems

Make transparencies of poems. Have children come up to the overhead projector and find different letters, words, rhymes, patterns, etc. Your students will enjoy using this very grown-up machine.

✢ Play Spotlight

Turn off the lights in your room and give a student a flashlight. Have him or her turn on the flashlight and "spotlight" a particular word. This is a great activity for all levels of readers because you can choose the word according to each child's ability.

✢ Pocketful of Poems

Write each line of a poem on a sentence strip. Have the children work together to place the poem in the correct order in a pocket chart. Read it as a group to check for accuracy. This can also be done on a smaller basis by cutting up copies of the poem and placing the strips into an envelope. Students can put it back in order as a center activity and ask a friend to check it.

✢ Wait Your Turn, Please

Post a poem on the board, overhead, or easel and have girls and boys alternate reading lines. Read it again and switch the order of readers.

✢ Calling All Readers

Assign each child a different line of a poem you have written on chart paper and give him or her time to practice reading it. Once everyone is comfortable with his or her part, you can have a community read. (A community read is one where everyone participates by reading aloud the specific line of the poem he or she has practiced. Everyone has a chance to read and feels successful in doing so.)

✢ Pointers, Please

Throughout the course of the year, give each student an opportunity to come to the front of the class and point to the words with a pointer while the rest of the class reads the poem aloud.

Activity Suggestions and Ideas (cont.)

⁛ Go Van Gogh

This activity will last almost the whole year. Each week ask one child to illustrate the poem on which you are working. Keep the pages and create a class book of student-illustrated poetry that can be showcased at an end-of-the-year-literacy night.

⁛ Fraction Attraction

Use this idea after you have introduced fractions in your math curriculum. First, have the children count how many letters are in the poem you have selected. That number acts as your denominator. Then have half of the children count vowels and half of them count consonants. These numbers will be the numerators in your fractions. The total number of vowels over the total number of letters makes a fraction. Repeat the process with consonants.

⁛ Guesses, Please

A great way to strengthen students' estimation skills is to have them guess how many of a certain thing there are in a poem. For example, students can guess how many consonants, vowels, words, or letters a poem contains. Estimates can be put into a jar during the course of the week and the answer can be decided on Friday, as a class.

⁛ Graph-a-ma-taph

Another enjoyable tie between math and literacy can be made by having students graph the number of sight words, vowels, consonants, individual letters of the alphabet, etc., there are in a poem. Groups of students can be responsible for counting different things and entering the information onto a giant class graph. Questions from you will give children practice with data interpretation. This activity can be tailored to specific needs or to review curriculum pieces already taught.

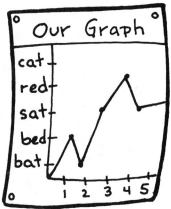

⁛ Units Unite

Some of the poems can be incorporated into a unit of study. This book contains pieces about insects, transportation, feelings, friendship, night, the New Year, and much more. Poems offer a plausible link between literacy and science or social studies topics.

⁛ Speech, Speech

Have each child choose a poem with which he or she is comfortable. After sufficient practice, he or she can dramatically read it in front of the class. This offers an excellent opportunity for reading with expression and with an audience in mind.

Activity Suggestions and Ideas *(cont.)*

✛ Word Frames

Purchase a small, inexpensive picture frame ahead of time (or borrow one from home). Give it to a child during whole- or small-group time and ask him or her to come up to the chart and frame a particular word. You can challenge your strong readers and target areas of difficulty for your beginning readers depending upon which word you ask him or her to frame.

✛ Start Your Stories, Please

Use the titles of the poems as inspirational writing prompts. Your students can write about what they do on a sleepover, describe their own grown-up wishes, recount a trip they've taken—the possibilities go on and on.

✛ Authors—On Your Marks

Some of the poems lend themselves to being re-written. An easy way to get your students into writing poetry is to use poetry blanks. Retype a poem, leaving occasional blank spaces. (Be sure to keep the rhythm of the poem.) Let the children fill in their own ideas in each blank. As they get better at this, the blank spaces can be positioned in more challenging ways.

✛ Lights, Camera, Action!

Many of the poems open up the possibility for companion actions. You may find that as you read a poem aloud for the second or third time, your students invent actions to go along with the words. If not, brainstorm a set of actions that would be appropriate for the poem and practice them. You can do a "final performance" for a neighboring class or another faculty member in the school once your children are comfortable with their parts.

✛ Fluency For All

For this activity, you will be in charge of the pointer and the children will read the poem aloud as you point. Tell them that they must keep pace with the pointer at all times. Move the pointer at an appropriate pace for your students. If you pause, so must they. If you speed up, they must as well. Your students will find it amusing if you slow down or speed up considerably during this activity.

✛ Technology Too

Using a painting or drawing program, have your children illustrate the week's poem on a computer. If you transfer the poem to chart paper and display it in your room, the illustrations done by the children can make a border around it. It will be a wonderful addition to your room or hallway that will make your technology coordinator proud.

Activity Suggestions and Ideas *(cont.)*

✛ Books, Books, Books

Make a poem into a book by typing each line or phrase on its own page. Staple or bind the pages together in the correct order and let each child illustrate his or her own or have groups of children work on pages together to make a class big book that everyone can read.

✛ ABC

Have your students highlight a pre-determined list of words in a poem. Then ask them to write the words in alphabetical order beneath it. Start with just a few words at a time then increase the difficulty by adding more words and words that begin with the same letter.

✛ Sticky-Note Cover-Up

This activity allows for a terrific amount of individualized instruction. You will need to reproduce the poem you want to use onto a piece of chart paper before starting. Give each child a small sticky note. Once each child has a note, call him or her up to the chart and ask him or her to cover up a specific word. For your shy or less able students, initially choose words you are certain they will know. As they become more comfortable with the group and the process, increase the difficulty of the words you give. For your more proficient readers, select words that only appear once or that do not follow phonemic rules. They will enjoy the challenge.

✛ Word Ladders

You'll need a reproducible pattern of a ladder for this activity. A hand-drawn one will work just as well as a pre-made picture. Write a key word from the poem you are using on the top rung of the ladder and make enough copies for each student in your room to have his or her own. In each of the rungs of the ladder, ask your students to write words that rhyme with the word at the top of the ladder. As your children gain confidence, the ladders can get longer.

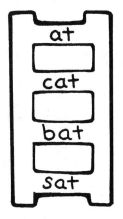

✛ Handful of Letters

Have your students trace their hands on blank pieces of paper. Provide each student with a word to write in the palm of the traced hand. Their job is to write one rhyming word in each of the fingers. This activity is good for challenging and reviewing, depending on your needs.

Student Book Cover

Pattern Pages

Note to teachers: Enlarge the patterns below and on page 11 as needed. Some of them can be used with more than one poem!

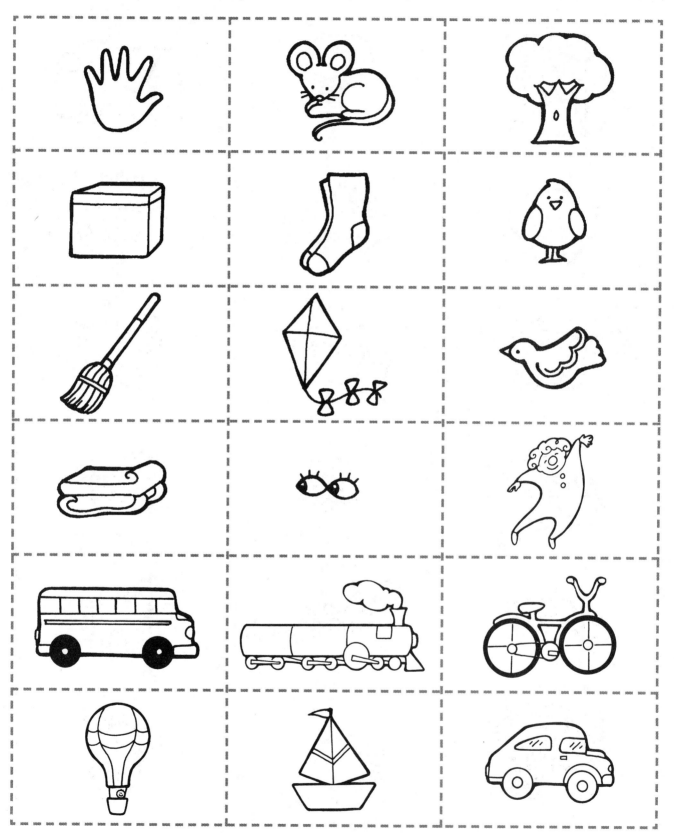

Pattern Pages *(cont.)*

Note to teachers: Enlarge the patterns below and on page 10 as needed. Some of them can be used with more than one poem!

Adding

Two and two
gives you four.
Two and three
makes one more.

One and two
gives you three.
You and me
makes a "we"!

All Of Us

Some of us can jump.
Some of us can wink.
Some of us can run,
but all of us can think.

Some of us go fast.
Some can take a while.
Some of us are shy,
but all of us can smile.

Some of us will start.
Some of us will end.
Some of us are in between,
but all of us are friends.

Almost Five

When I am old,
like maybe six,
I'll be too old,
to play with sticks.

When I am old,
like nine or eight,
I'll be too old,
to run or skate.

When I am old,
like almost ten,
I'll be too old,
to have fun then.

But when I'm five,
I'll be just right,
To ride or jump,
or fly my kite.

At Recess

Ten will jump,
Nine will run,
Eight will play,
Beneath the sun.

Seven hop,
Six will skip,
Five will play,
Snap the Whip.

Four will ride,
Three will fly,
Two will give
The swings a try.

One will stop
and will say,
"Would you like
to come and play?"

Be A Friend

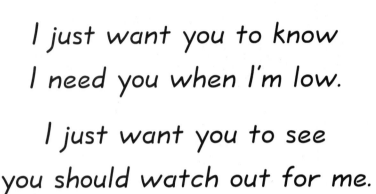

I just want you to know
I need you when I'm low.

I just want you to see
you should watch out for me.

I just want you to say,
"Would you come out and play?"

I just want you to ride
bikes with me side by side.

I just want you to walk
outside so we could talk.

I just want you to ask
if I'll help with a task.

I just want you to think
I'd like a smile and a wink.

I just want you to be a friend.

Before Bed

Tell me a story,
sing me a song,
give me a smile,
to hold all night long.

Tell me again,
sing me a tune,
give me a dream,
to take to the moon.

Bug and Bee

Once there was a little bug,

her legs were white and black.

She had two big orange wings,

and a spot upon her back.

She liked to eat the long green grass,

and fly around the trees.

And she was friends with all she met,

except the yellow bees.

But one day as she flew around,

she saw a small bee crying.

She sat down next to him and said,

"I'll help you with your flying!"

Pretty soon, bee was up in flight

saying, "Thank you little one!"

From that day on, they were best of friends,

always having fun.

Come Out

Come out little one,
come here and play!
Come out little one,
do what I say.

Come out little one,
come see me run.
Come out little one,
Let's find the sun.

Come out little one,
come jump and spin.
Come out little one,
or I'll come in!

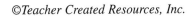

Encouragement

One, one,
I can run.

Two, two,
so can you.

Three, three,
follow me.

Four, four,
run some more.

Five, five,
stay alive.

Six, six,
do some tricks.

Friends

They are round,
they are square.

They are here,
they are there.

They will give,
they will take.

They will buy,
they will make.

They can help,
they can share.
They can laugh,
they can care.

Funny

It is funny to be blue.

It is funny to be red.

It is funny to be upside down,

Just standing on your head.

It is funny to be yellow.

It is funny to be pink.

It is funny to be inside out,

And that is what I think!

Grown-Up Wishes

When I grow up
I want to be,
Much taller than
my daddy's knee.

When I grow up
I want to buy,
one hundred candies,
just to try.

When I grow up
I want to write,
a word that is not
spelled just right.

When I grow up
I want to say:
I will not eat
my peas today!

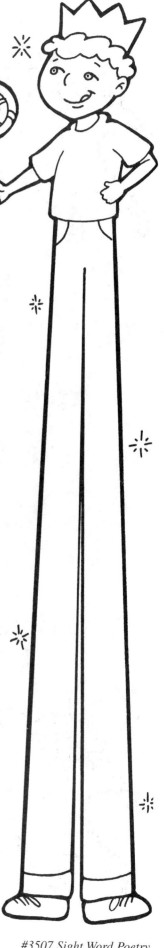

Guessing Game

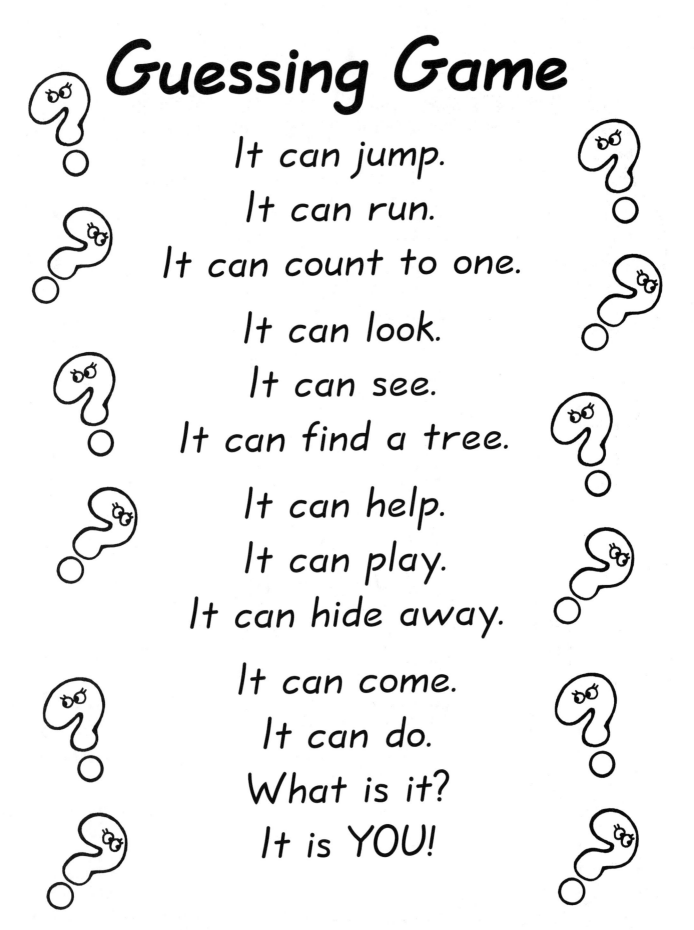

It can jump.
It can run.
It can count to one.

It can look.
It can see.
It can find a tree.

It can help.
It can play.
It can hide away.

It can come.
It can do.
What is it?
It is YOU!

Hide and Seek

Ten go in,
nine go under,
eight go up,
seven wonder.

Six go over,
five go down,
four go out,
three just frown.

Two go out
and all around.
One stays put
without a sound.

none are found.

I Like, I Can

I like pink.

I like brown.

I can see a funny clown.

I like blue.

I like red.

I can jump upon my bed.

I like orange.

I like gray.

I can fly my kite today.

I like green.

I like black.

I can eat up all my snack.

I Saw It

Once I saw a yellow fish,
under the deep blue sea.
Then I saw a fat green frog,
who jumped right over me.

Next I saw a little red bird
just flying around his house.
Then I saw an orange cat,
eating one black mouse.

And I saw a pretty white dog,
riding in a car.
Then a funny purple bug,
he could walk so far.

There is one thing I did not see
among so many things
I'd be glad if I could say
I'd seen a cow with wings!

Just Because

I like to slide
when I ride.

I like to blink
when I think.

I like to talk
when I walk.

I like to speed
when I read.

And I like to sing
when I swing.

But I do not like to leap
when I sleep.

Just Like Me

Just like "this"
or just like "that".
Oh me, oh my, oh dear!

Just like "him"
or just like "her".
That is all I hear!

Just like "some"
or just like "one".
Who says it has to be?

Just like "you"
or just like "them".
Well how 'bout just like ME?

Let's See

(Sharing with a Crocodile)

One for you
and three for me.
I think that's fine,
or should it be...

One for you
and five for me.
Yes, yes, that's fair,
but, hmm, let's see...

One for you
and TEN for me.
That is just right,
don't you agree?

My Tree

Up in my tree,
that's where I'll be.
Up in my tree,
where I can see.

Up in my tree,
that's big and brown.
Up in my tree,
I'll not come down.

Up in my tree,
I like to play.
Up in my tree,
I stay all day.

Up in my tree,
the sky is blue.
Up in my tree,
will you come too?

Not!

Not one, not two.
Not red, not blue.

Not up, not down.
Not green, not brown.

Not small, not big.
Not zag, not zig.
Not me, not you.
Not us, then who?

Opposites

When I am up,
you are down.
When I smile,
you frown.

When I am first,
you are last.
When I am slow,
you are fast.

When I am in,
you are out.
When I'm a whisper,
you're a shout.

But when I'm happy,
so are you,
because it's just
more fun with two!

Practicing

I can count,
want to see?
Four, two, one, three!

I can count,
it is fun.
Two, four, three, one!

I can count,
a little more.
Three, two, one, four!

I can count,
just wait, you.
One...three...four...two!

Pretending

Where will I go?
Will I find a star?
Where will I go?
Will it be very far?

Where will I go?
Will it take me long?
Where will I go?
Will I sing a song?

Where will I go?
Will I jump and play?
Where will I go?
Will I want to stay?

Where will I go?
Will I make a friend?
Where will I go?
What fun to pretend!

The New Year

This year when I clean my room,
This year I will use a broom.

This year I will eat my dinner.
This year I will be a winner.

This year I will read and write.
This year I'll try not to fight.

This year I will say nice things.
This year I will smile and sing.

This year I will run and play.
This year I will work each day.

This year I will do my best.
This year I will love the rest.

The Sleepover

We jump,
we sing,
we run and play.

We draw,
we laugh,
we build with clay.

We eat,
we ride,
we dance and creep.

We think,
we wish,
and then—we sleep.

The Story

Once I saw a small, white cat
a crown upon her head.
Once I ran into a goat
who had a beard of red.

Once I went to see a frog
who liked to read and write.
Once I had a chance to meet
a fish who sang all night.

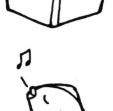

Once I may have even seen
a duck who played the flute.
But I've never come across
a horse who wears a suit —
Have you?

The Story Teller

Come with me
and you will find,
a little fun –
don't fall behind!

Come with me
and you will fly,
just like a bird
up in the sky.

Come with me
and you will look,
at all the joy
found in a book.

Come with me
and you will say,
"Can I come back
another day?"

The Trip

Let's use our feet
and see who we meet.

Let's ride a bike
to a place that we like.

Let's hop a train
for a trip to Maine.

Let's catch a bus
without any fuss.

Let's get a boat
and float in the moat.

Let's start the car
then drive near and far.

Let's fly balloons
all the way to the moon.

Let's find a jet
and see where we get.

OR we could stay home
and pretend to roam.

The Wish

Make me big,
make me old.
Make me funny,
find me gold.

Make me small,
make me blue.
Make me magic,
just like you!

Things I Think

I'd like to know who,
would want to be blue.

I like to eat Jello®,
when I'm dressed in yellow.

I like a sled,
or a hat of red.

I like the night,
with its stars of white.

I like to be seen,
with eyes of green.

And I like to stay,
away from gray.

But most of all,
I like to think,
about being pink.

Tree House Rules

Come in here,
go out there.
Be a friend,
always share.

Give a bit,
clean your mess.
Bring a snack,
do your best.

When Are We Going?

"When are we going?"
Said the frog to the bee.
"When are we going?"
Said the dog to his flea.

"When are we going?"
The fly would ask the cat.
"When are we going?"
Said the spider to the bat.

"When are we going?"
The ant just had to say.
"When are we going?"
Said the bug in the hay?

"WHERE are we going?"
Said the mice to them all.
They had to stop and think,
but no one could recall.

Where Is The Cat?

Where is the cat?
Is she under the box?
Where is the cat?
Is she in the old socks?

Where is the cat?
Is she out on the car?
Where is the cat?
Is she up on a star?

Where is the cat?
Is she up in a tree?
Where is the cat?
She is sitting on me!

(now, where is the dog?)

Who Are You?

Who are you?

Are you a little black fly?

Who are you?

Are you wet or are you dry?

Who are you?

Are you fast like me?

Who are you?

Are you brown like a tree?

Who are you?

Do you walk or maybe run?

Who are you?

Can you count past one?

Who are you?

Wish Upon A Star

When I see a star,
I wish for many things.
When I see a star,
I wish that I had wings.

When I see a star,
I wish for love and joys.
When I see a star,
I wish for girls and boys.

When I see a star,
I wish for happy faces.
When I see a star,
I wish for special places.

You Can!

You can be little.
You can be big.
You can be pink,
just like a pig.

You can be yellow.
You can be brown.
You can be funny,
just like a clown.

You can be great,
like a queen or a king.
Yes, you can be
'most ANYTHING!